CITY OF THE DEAD
A Guide to Glasgow's Southern Necropolis

CITY OF THE DEAD
A Guide to Glasgow's Southern Necropolis

South Glasgow Heritage Environment Trust

Illustrations by Adrian B McMurchie

Dedicated to the memory of Charlotte Hutt

© South Glasgow Heritage Environment Trust 2007
ISBN 978-0-906169-65-0

Published by
Culture and Sport Glasgow
The Mitchell Library
North Street
Glasgow G3 7DN

Printed By Montgomery Litho Group, Glasgow

Contents

Introduction

Welcome to the City of the Dead – A Guide to Glasgow's Southern Necropolis. Please enjoy your visit. For your own safety please follow the route marked on this guide. It will take approximately 1.5 hours to follow the Heritage Trail from the Gatehouse and back again. Please remember at all times that this is a cemetery. The Southern Necropolis is hallowed ground which contains the remains of around 250,000 people and as such should be treated respectfully.

The foundation of the Southern Necropolis

The appalling condition of the Old Gorbals Burial Ground on Rutherglen Road (now the Rose Garden) and the method of internment employed there had long been the subject of public condemnation. Finally, at a public meeting held in the Baronial Hall on 15 November 1839, a proposal was put forward for the establishment of a new graveyard. At a second meeting held on 27 February 1840 the proposal was passed and a committee formed to launch the scheme. A prospectus was published that promised to bring the cost of owning a burial place within the reach of the poorest in society.

The seven acres of land which forms the central section was purchased from Glasgow merchant William Gilmour of Oatlands House on land that once formed part of the estate of Little Govan. The price of a lair would vary by its length and breadth and by its position within the grounds and repayment of the final sum was taken in weekly instalments at a minimum of sixpence per week. The price of the lairs was as follows:

Lair 7 ft x 3ft £1.1s
Lair 10 ft x 3ft £1.10s
Wall lair 10½ ft x 7½ ft £9
Wall lair 10½ ft x 10 ft £12
Lair within the central hedge 7 ft x 3 ft £1.16s
Lair within the central hedge 10 ft x 3 ft £2.12s.6d

The Southern Necropolis was officially opened in July 1840 and the first burial, that of the 16 month old daughter of Archibald Cochran took place on 21 July. By 1846 all the lairs of the central section were sold and a further two and a half acres at a price of £2063 was purchased from William Gilmour to form the eastern section. The following year an additional one and a quarter acres was purchased at a cost of £1000. The demand for lairs continued and in 1850 nine and a half acres of land at a cost of £4858 was purchased from the Trustees of George Jardine, former Professor of Logic at the College of Glasgow, to form the western section. The City of Glasgow took over responsibility for the Southern Necropolis in 1952. For a more detailed account of the founding of the Southern Necropolis readers are advised to borrow a copy of the book *The City of the Dead* by Charlotte Hutt from their local library.

Guide to the Southern Necropolis

The monuments in the Southern Necropolis are mostly Victorian and form part of a unique record of the architectural development of monumental sculpture of the period. Many monuments have been unable to withstand the elements due to unsuitable construction

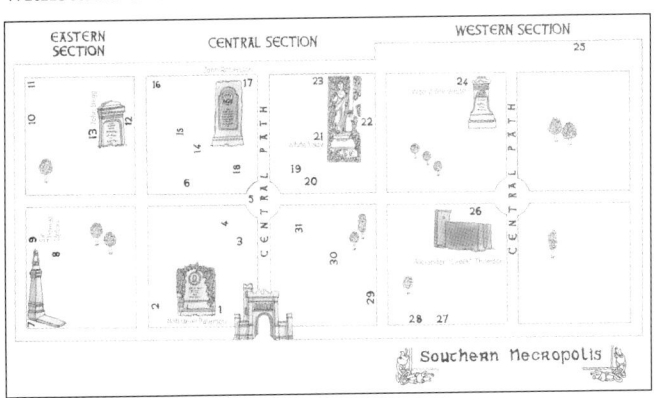

materials but others have survived the passing years relatively unscathed and their elaborate architectural design merits recognition on an artistic and cultural basis. The rise in interest in family history has fostered a greater public awareness of our graveyards and this has resulted in recognition of their economic value, particularly in tourism, as thousands of people visit Glasgow each year to research their ancestry. This alone should assist local authorities to engage with local communities to protect, preserve and restore a much-neglected part of our heritage.

When most people undertake research into their family history they are likely to pay a visit to a graveyard where, if they are lucky, they will discover a monument with information about their relatives. Not all graves have monuments. Some may have been broken and removed by the local authority for reasons of health and safety. Others may have been vandalised with the broken pieces lying scattered around the graveyard.

The Southern Necropolis, like many graveyards, has a variety of monuments by which we can distinguish the evolution of architectural style and design. Unlike its close neighbour, the Old Gorbals Burial Ground on Rutherglen Road, which was opened in 1715 and has many examples of gravestones with emblems of trade carved upon them, the Southern Necropolis owes its interest to the work of Victorian sculptors and masons.

As you enter the Southern Necropolis through the impressive castellated Norman-style gatehouse built by Charles Wilson in 1848 you will be facing the central path of the central section. There are directional markers around the graveyard to indicate the graves, especially those of particular interest, thereby making your route round the graveyard easier.

Welcome to the Southern Necropolis – Your tour starts here…

Having passed through the Charles Wilson gatehouse turn left and walk towards the first directional marker on your left.

This granite pedestal tomb set against the outer wall has an impressive bronze portrait bust and is the resting place of…

1   Dr Nathaniel Paterson (1787-1871) Disruption Minister

The eldest son of Walter Paterson, stone engraver of Balmaclellan and Mary Locke, Nathaniel Paterson was born on 3 July 1787 at Kells in Kirkcudbright. His Grand-father was Robert Paterson, a staunch supporter of the Covenanters who had made it his mission in life to travel the countryside setting up and repairing memorials to Covenanters. The eponymous hero of Sir Walter Scott's Old Mortality was modelled on Robert Paterson. Nathaniel studied

divinity at Edinburgh. On leaving he tutored at Lilburn Tower in Northumberland until he was ordained at Galashiels on 30 August 1821 where he was appointed by the local land-owners against the wishes of the congregation. However, he managed to win them over and on 8 February 1825 he married Margaret Laidlaw (1800-1864) and they remained in Galashiels until the Magistrates and Town Council of Glasgow offered him the position of minister at St Andrews Church next to Glasgow Green.

The Treaty of Union in 1707 guaranteed there would be no interference in the governance of the Church of Scotland but by 1712 Parliament had re-introduced the practice of 'patronage'. This meant that the choice of a congregation could be overruled by the local land-owners, magistrates or town councillors.

Nathaniel took up his charge on 20 February 1834 in the face of stiff opposition and resentment from his congregation. This time it seemed he could please no one. He was constantly patronised by the more traditional members of the congregation who wanted him removed. Once again he managed to win over the congregation but by 1843 things came to a head and those who could no longer accept the control lay patrons imposed on church appointments swept out of the General Assembly and declared themselves the Free Church of Scotland.

On 18 May 1843, the day of the Disruption in the Church of Scotland, Nathaniel, his brother the Reverend Walter Paterson and their friend Dr Landsborough were among the procession of clergy who made their way from St Andrew's Church in Edinburgh to

Tanfield Hall to sign the Act of Separation and Deed of Demission. On his return to Glasgow almost his entire congregation came out in support and together they joined the Free Church of Scotland. They worshipped in the hall of the Black Bull Inn on Trongate until 1844 when a new Church was opened in Hanover Square.

Paterson was appointed Moderator of the General Assembly of the Free Church in 1850. He had many an interest outside his ministry and is said to have been the inventor of the Riddle Lifeboat. His published works include *The Manse Garden* (Glasgow 1836) and *The Cry of the Perishing* (Edinburgh 1842). He died at Helensburgh on 25 April 1871. In David Octaves Hill's famous painting of the Disruption ministers the Reverend Nathaniel Paterson DD can be recognised sitting in front of the left pillar.

Dead You Know?

The Southern Necropolis contains over 250,000 burials with the size of the three sections totalling 21 acres. The word 'Necropolis' comes from the Greek 'nekros' meaning 'death' and 'polis' meaning 'city'.

Continue along and follow the path around to the next directional marker on the right. Here you will find the obelisk monument that marks the grave of…

2   Peter Ferguson (1801-1885)
Missionary for temperance

Peter Ferguson found his voice for temperance while working in a local wood yard where he saw many of his fellow workers suffering from the effects of too much alcohol. His preaching often led to accusations of fanaticism but his fervour also led to others embracing temperance. He engaged in gospel addresses throughout the city and became a 'missionary' on behalf of the Gorbals Total Abstinence Society. He assisted Robert Drummond and others in setting up the Band of Hope in Glasgow in November 1870, which later became the Scottish Band of Hope Union with over 650 societies throughout Scotland. The Band of Hope specialised in presenting the message of Temperance as emotionally as possible in the hope of swaying the young towards total abstinence.

The message of temperance was broadcast through the use of song, stories and illustrations which were full of images of starving families and weeping women and repentant deathbed scenes. At many of their concerts and soirees, their songs and lantern lectures were accompanied by cakes and soft drinks which proved particularly attractive to their young target audience. They provided Christmas treats and Sunday picnics, often held in halls in cold dark streets where cakes and treats were rare. The objective of the temperance movement was the 'absolute prohibition of the manufacture, importation and sale of all intoxicating liquors to be used as a beverage'. 'Signing the Pledge' may have helped to save many individuals and families from a lot of unhappiness. Ferguson was an elder at

Renfield Street Free Church (where British Homes Stores is now) and in later life became known as Father Ferguson. He died as a result of an accident at the ripe old age of 84 in 1885.

Dead You Know?

> Obelisks are constructed with a square bottom section on top of a brick base with a tapering shaft of stone and a pyramidal top. They were erected to people of some importance such as surgeons, doctors, architects, etc and by the Victorian period they outrivaled most other monuments in height. Obelisks have a tendency to shift on their brick base and often tilt to one side and will eventually collapse if they are not repositioned on a stable foundation. The Southern Necropolis has many examples of obelisk monuments and they can be seen from almost anywhere along the route.

Return along the path to the central path in front of the gatehouse. If you decide to cross between the stones then be careful and watch your footing. Walk along the central path to the next directional marker, on the left hand side. You will be directed to the grave marker between the stones that marks the headstone of…

3 Thomas Bollen Seath (1820-1903) Shipbuilder

Seath was born on the 20 September 1820 in Prestonpans, East Lothian. His father was an employee of a coastal shipping company. At the age of five Thomas permanently injured his spine in an accident.

At eight he moved with his parents to Glasgow where he attended school until the age of 14 when he gained employment as a cabin boy on one of the steamers that sailed between Glasgow and Liverpool. The young Seath served nearly five years at Thomson and McConnell's Steamers in Liverpool, Belfast and the North Highlands. Later he became clerk of the Largs Steamboat Company and despite continual health problems worked and studied to gain qualifications in ship management and operation. Thomas started his own shipbuilding yard at Meadowside, Partick at the mouth of the river Kelvin in 1853. In 1856 he moved to Rutherglen where he built, owned and even operated the small steamer *Artizan*, which had pioneering engine controls on the bridge, between Rutherglen and Glasgow. However the increasing business at his shipbuilding yard meant he had to abandon his successful steamer business. He designed and built the first six Cluthas, small steamships of shallow draft – marine omnibuses that ferried workmen up and down river.

The age of the Clutha came to an end at the turn of the century with the construction of the subway and competition from the world's largest tramway network. Seath built steamships for Loch Lomond and Loch Maree, Windermere and Ullswater. He also constructed steam yachts – *The Fairy* for the King of Burma and the *Little Eastern* for the King of Siam, both commissioned in 1872. Almost all of the ships he produced were iron-hulled and this proved to be a factor in their longevity. An example is the *Esperance* built in 1869 and the *Raven* built in 1871, both of which are in the Windermere Steamboat Collection. Thomas

Bollen Seath was a major influence in the design and production of high quality small ships and the shipyard that he leased for 47 years from Rutherglen Corporation finally ceased when access to the sea was closed off by a weir at Glasgow Green. By then it had built over 300 ships, including the paddle steamer *Isle of Arran*.

In 1864, Seath bought 'The Oaks' at Langbank which he renamed 'Sunny Oaks' and in that year he hired the services of Alexander 'Greek' Thomson to design a new art gallery-cum-music room and a new lodge at the property. Thomas Bollen Seath passed away at 'Sunny Oaks' on the 3 February 1903. The cottage was demolished in 1974.

Return to the central path and continue to the next directional marker on the left. Again you will be directed between the stones, to the blonde sandstone headstone of…

4   William S Williams (1790-1842) Actor

Better known by the stage name of 'Scotch Williams', he was born in Glasgow in 1790. In his early years he was a favourite actor at the Theatres Royal in Dublin, Bath, Bristol, Liverpool and Birmingham. For a number of years he performed at the Haymarket in London. Latterly, on account of his declining health, he trod the boards at smaller venues. His final performance was at Sadler's Wells in June 1842. He returned to his cottage in Kilmarnock Road on the outskirts of Glasgow where he died on the 2 August 1842 (probably from arteriolosclerosis). He was survived by his wife Jean Stewart. They had no children.

The headstone and footstone were originally a pair of lair markers. Headstones rose to popularity in the 18th century; the earliest examples being small and limited in surface area and providing only the name and date of death. Most of the stones from this period were made from sandstone and over time have fared badly from the elements. 19th century headstones can be distinguished by their larger size and vary enormously not only by their style and design but also by the variety of materials used such as slate, sandstone, granite and marble. Many 19th century headstones are mounted on a pedestal and surmounted by a finial.

Over time the base becomes loosened and the monument can be easily toppled by vandals or high winds. This particular headstone has the added Greek emblem of two downward facing torches with flame extinguished symbolising the end of earthly life. Flaming torches facing upward represent eternal life. Torches usually appear in pairs.

Dead You Know?

Spread throughout the different monuments, and sometimes resembling crusts of white or blue paint, is a fascinating plant called lichen. The plant consists of two types of organism in one, where cells of algae are inside fungal strands. Cells of algae provide the plant with food and absorb energy from the sun just like other plants. Cemeteries and churchyards across Britain have been found to contain over 100 species of lichen.

Return the way you came to the central path and walk to the central circle. Here you will find the recent re-interment of 20 individuals whose remains were discovered at an archaeological dig in the High Street...

5 Franciscan Re-interment

The Franciscans arrived in Glasgow in the early 14th century and built their first chapel in the area where George Street now stands. A Franciscan presence remained until around 1559 when the Reformation led to their suppression. They did not re-establish themselves in the city until 1868 when they set up a small mission in Calton. In the same year the mission purchased a piece of land in Cumberland Street, Gorbals and on the 13 December 1868 they opened a temporary chapel which became known as Greyfriars.

The succeeding years saw the parish in the Gorbals prosper and grow and it was soon recognised that a larger chapel was needed. Funds were raised and lodged with the Glasgow City Bank. The money raised for the building work was lost when the Glasgow City Bank collapsed. New funds were raised but the original design by the famous architect Peter Paul Pugin was altered. The first turf was turned on the 2 February 1880 closely followed by a ceremony to lay the foundation

stone. The formal opening of the chapel took place on the 1 June 1881.

During an archaeological excavation in 2005 at the site for the new City Science Centre on High Street the remains of twenty individuals, who are generally thought to be lay members of the order of St Francis, were discovered. Another notable discovery found during the excavations was the original well of the friary, the opening of which was surrounded by a perfectly crafted circle of stones. The well itself is to become a key feature of a planned medieval garden to be created on the north edge of the site, near to George Street. The Archbishop of Glasgow, the Most Reverend Mario Conti, conducted a mass at St Andrews Cathedral, after which Rev Patrick Lonsdale of the Order of St Francis and Guardian of the Glasgow Franciscan Friary in the Gorbals, respectfully transferred the remains to the Southern Necropolis for the graveside committal. It was fitting that, with strong links to the Gorbals, the re-interment should take place at the Southern Necropolis.

Standing at the central circle with your back to the gatehouse turn left and walk towards 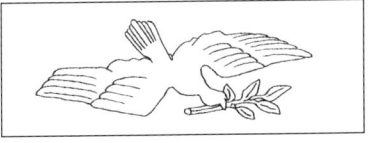 the eastern section. On the right just before the next marker you will notice an ornate high medieval style Celtic cross belonging to Robert Bruce and family. (Not King Robert the Bruce!). Further along you will find a marker on your right pointing in the direction of an obelisk. This obelisk with symbolic dove representing the Holy Spirit marks the resting place of…

6 Malcolm MacFarlane (1810-1862) Chartist

Malcolm MacFarlane was a cabinetmaker and trade unionist as well as one of the leaders of the Glasgow Chartist movement.

The principles of Chartism can be traced to the radicalism of earlier movements and demands for social and political reform. In the early 19th century traditional craft industries were facing decline from increasing competition from machinery. Many workers were forced to find employment in the exploitative regime of the factories where they faced long hours on low wages. The introduction of the Corn Law in 1815 only served to maintain food prices at an artificially high level and depress domestic markets resulting in periods of high unemployment. It was common knowledge that the electoral system was corrupt and that power was bestowed on the wealthy. Disillusionment with the behaviour of the Whig Government confirmed the belief that the lack of the vote led to exploitation and hardship. It was Chartism's aim to end this exploitation.

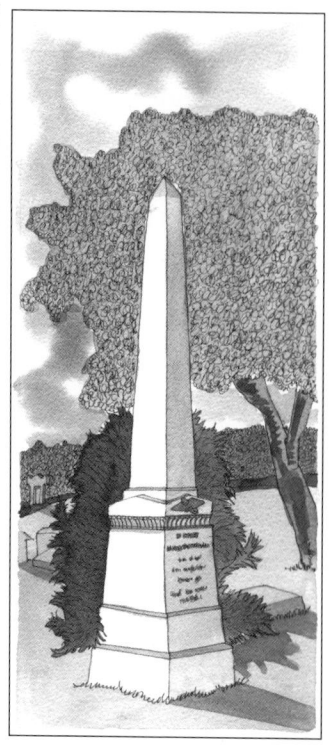

Chartism arose out of the failure of the 1832 Reform Act to extend the vote beyond the middle classes. In June 1836 the London Working Men's Association (LWMA) was founded and at a meeting in 1838 it drew up a document for political change called the 'People's Charter'. The charter, from which the movement took its name, called for the reform of the electoral system and had six main points, which were; a vote for all males aged 21 and over; a secret ballot; no property qualification for members of parliament; payment for all members of parliament; constituencies of equal size and annual parliaments.

As Chartism's message spread throughout the industrial regions of Britain, Malcolm MacFarlane became a prominent speaker at mass meetings. On 28 June 1838, a crowd of 100,000 people gathered at Glasgow Green to hear Chartist speakers. In 1839, he became vice-president of the Glasgow Universal Suffrage Association and in 1842 joined the Glasgow Complete Suffrage Association of which he also became vice-president. He was particularly involved with the growth of the Chartist Churches, set up to spread the message of social justice, and presided at the first service of the first church in Glasgow's High Street in September 1839. His zeal for moral and physical education made him one of the most popular Chartist preachers. He was a strong supporter of the movement to abstain from all excisable articles not only because it attacked the establishment's financial power, but because like other early socialists he saw alcohol abuse as a trap for the working man.

When the Chartist organisation collapsed he continued to work for the fledgling temperance movement and for the abolition of slavery. Above all he strove to make people aware that the improvement in standards of living and labour for working people depended on their ability to work together. Malcolm MacFarlane died on 20 February 1862, aged 52 years.

From Malcolm MacFarlane's obelisk continue towards the eastern section and turn to your left on entry. A few yards along on the right is the impressively large blonde sandstone obelisk of the White family. Follow the path round to the right where, on the right hand side, you will notice the large granite Celtic cross with intricately carved knotwork in memory of Christina McKinlay.

Dead you Know?

The cross was not used in the design of monuments until the 19th century and very rarely does it appear as a symbolic carving. Before this period it was seen as a Catholic emblem and its use was to be avoided. It rose to popularity in the more secular 19th and 20th centuries, not only as a monument but also as a decorative element on many monuments. Crosses come in various designs, for example: white marble to mark the grave of a child, high medieval style and Celtic, all of which can be made of either sandstone or granite.

Return to the trail and walk forward. On the left side of the path you will notice a blonde sandstone headstone to the memory of Captain John C Ewing, who was lost at sea in 1857, which bears the anchor emblem of a mariner or fisherman but can also represent a message of hope. Straight ahead towards the left corner you will see a directional marker marking the grave of…

7   Agnes Harkness (1771-1856) Heroine of Matagorda

Agnes is recorded on the monument to her husband James Reston, a sergeant in the British (Scots Brigade) 94th Regiment of Foot. Her actions are detailed in a rare book entitled *The Eventful Life of a Soldier*. Agnes and her four-year-old son, like many families at this time, accompanied the men on campaign. In this case to the small fort of Matagorda, part of the outlying defences of Cadiz, the capital of free Spain, during the Peninsular War. While under bombardment from 30 French cannon, Agnes took her son to the shelters and returned to aid the surgeon in the dressing of the wounded. The surgeon ordered a drummer boy to brave the battery and fetch water from the well. On seeing the boy hesitate, Agnes grabbed the water bucket and ventured out into the battery. As she was about to lower the bucket into the well a piece of shot severed the rope but with the help of a sailor she managed to retrieve the situation. Between intervals in the French bombardment she carried sandbags to help in the repair of the battery. She handed out ammunition to the troops and supplied them with wine and water.

The regiment held out until 21 April when their ammunition finally ran out. Agnes took her place beside the troops on the battery for the final assault. Realising that the fort's defences had almost collapsed the French sent out a strong force to take the fort. Determined to fire a farewell volley, the men of the 94th crammed their three cannon with powder, ball, and anything else at hand. As the French closed to within 300 yards the regiment fired their last into the heart of the French troops, forcing them to flee. The order to withdraw was given by General Graham on the 22 April 1810. During their withdrawal Agnes made three forays across the battery, amid shot and shell, to retrieve her son and their belongings.

Agnes returned with her son to Glasgow and on his discharge from the army her husband joined them, where they lived on his small army pension of 1s 10d a day (about 8p). At the instigation of officers, for her heroic actions at Matagorda, she was persuaded to represent her case for a pension to the commander-in-chief. With his full support her case was recommended to the Secretary of State for War. The request was refused on the grounds of insufficient funds. The whereabouts of her son who had also joined the army was unclear. When her husband died on the 24 October 1834, Agnes descended into poverty and destitution. She found herself in the Glasgow Poorhouse where she occupied the position of sick nurse when required.

In 1845, her plight was brought to public attention through a report in the local press and an appeal was raised on her behalf. The appeal raised enough funds to present a pension of £30 a year to give Agnes the security she richly deserved. She spent the remainder of her life in comfort in the Town Hospital, where she paid for her board out of the annuity raised by a generous public. After setting aside funds for her funeral she generously made donations to charitable causes. Agnes Harkness passed away after a short illness on the 24 December 1856, aged 85 years.

Just a few stones along on the right is an interesting little monument in the form of an open book on a square block pedestal. This grey granite monument with symbolic clasped hands represents a 19th century sign of farewell and is in memory of M L Gilchrist from her fellow employees at Gibb and Hogg Ltd, Airdrie.

From there it is just a short walk to the next marker, on the right hand side where again you will be directed between the stones to the grave marker of…

8 William Cameron (1801-1877) Pawnbroker

The son of John Cameron and Jean McAdam, William was born in Dunipace, Stirlingshire on 3 December 1801 and there he spent the early years of his life. He was educated with the aim of joining the ministry. However, when William was 17 years old the death of his father ended any thoughts of the church as a career. Turning his attention to the teaching profession, he was appointed as a schoolmaster at Bathgate in 1826 and spent over 10 years in that position. Few details are recorded as to his success as a teacher but it was noted that he was greatly admired by his students and colleagues.

Around 1836 he moved to Glasgow where he became a pawnbroker and, later, the first Chairman of the Glasgow Pawnbrokers Association. He was known to have a love of music and song; evidence of which comes from a handwritten manuscript containing 56 songs and 50 poems including *Gourock Bay*, *My Ain Wife*, *Gowan Lea* and *Morag's Fairy Glen*. This glen is located to the south of Dunoon towards Innellan and was gifted to the town in 1929. It is a picturesque spot with walkways and bridges.

Return through the gravestones to the path and just ahead, on the right, there is a marker pointing to a draped urn on a square pedestal, in front of which is the coped stone monument of…

9   Sir Thomas Lipton (1850-1931) Grocer and Yachtsman

Thomas Lipton was born of Irish parentage at Crown Street, Gorbals in 1850. At the age of 10 years he was employed as a message boy at stationers A & W Kennedy and later with Tillie & Henderson, shirt manufacturers. He became a cabin boy and at the age of 15 he crossed the Atlantic to the United States, arriving at the time when the country was recovering from a brutal civil war. He soon found employment as an assistant in a grocer's store but it wasn't long before he grew homesick and returned to Glasgow with £100 in his pocket. He began to work in his parents' small shop in Crown Street and having tried unsuccessfully to coax his father into expansion he decided it was time to set up on his own.

Using the money he had made in the United States and the drive and ingenuity picked up along the way, he opened his first Lipton's Market on 10 May 1871 (his 21st birthday) at Stobcross Street, Anderston. His brilliantly lit shops shone like a beacon in the thick industrial smog that hung over Glasgow and attracted housewives looking for special offers. Thomas Lipton soon expanded his grocery empire into many corners of the United Kingdom.

His success was attributable to two factors; firstly, he cut out the middleman and bought directly from his suppliers, and secondly, while in the United States he had learned the art of advertising. He employed a commercial artist and together they devised a series of simple but ingenious posters that amused and delighted his customers.

In the 1880's he again set his sights on the United

States, a move which indirectly got him involved in the tea business. Again, he cut out the middleman and began buying tea plantations in Ceylon. The arrival of the coffee blight in 1878 had all but wiped out coffee production in what was regarded as a coffee-producing region. Land was cheap and within months Lipton had purchased five tea estates. Lipton's tea was set to rival coffee as the United States' favourite beverage. A life-long passion for sailing would lead him to become more widely known for his many unsuccessful attempts at regaining the America's Cup for Britain than for his business affairs.

In 1898 he was awarded a knighthood and had responded to public pressure to allow his business empire to become a limited company. There was such a huge interest in shares that the venture was over subscribed. Sir Thomas Lipton, who had made his first million by the age of 30, was created a baronet in 1902. He died aged 81 on 2 October 1931. In his will he left £80,000 to the poor of Glasgow and much more to the city's hospitals and institutions. The funeral cortege passed along Crown Street, where he was born, and thousands of mourners crowded the streets of Gorbals to say farewell.

Dead You Know?

The urn became a popular decorative top piece to headstones and pedestal tombs during the neo-classicist revival of the 19th century and continued throughout the Victorian era. The coped stone is a variation on the slab stone with a narrow raised central panel providing five raised surfaces for inscriptions and carvings.

Return to the path and continue forward and on through the path which joins from the right and all the way along to the next marker on your right side, which directs your attention to the grave of...

10 Archibald Sinclair (1850-1899)
Gaelic Printer

Archibald Sinclair was born 27 May 1850 the son of Archibald Sinclair founder of the Celtic Press in Glasgow. In 1862, aged 12 he attended the inaugural meeting of the Glasgow Islay Association with his father who was its founding President. He would later follow in his father's footsteps and become President of the Association which exists for the purpose of gathering and preserving the traditions, folk tales and poetry of Islay, and to bring together natives of the island who were resident in Glasgow.

He took over his father's role as head of the Celtic Press and continued to print and publish Gaelic books and to translate work from English into Gaelic. He became well-known for his anthology of Gaelic poetry called *An t-Òranaiche* (the Gaelic Songster) published between 1876 and 79. In later years the Sinclair Memorial Fund was set up with the aim of purchasing Gaelic literature to encourage the studying of Gaelic in Islay schools. The Directors offered to refund the fees of students of Islay descent who did well with their Gaelic studies at Glasgow High School Continuation Classes.

In 1925, the Glasgow Islay Association erected a monument to his memory at the family resting place in the Southern Necropolis. The inscription is in both English and Gaelic. The impressive broken Celtic cross belonging to it lies in pieces nearby.

As you return to the path the grey granite obelisk directly ahead of you in the corner marks the grave of...

11 James Cousland (1832-1866)
Architect

James Cousland was the son of Alexander Cousland and Elizabeth Stark. His family were prosperous wire manufacturers with a business in Mitchell Street, Glasgow. While articled to Charles Wilson (Southern Necropolis gatehouse 1848), Cousland met up with James Boucher, who was seven years' his senior, and together they formed a partnership in c1853. In 1857, they built for themselves a pair of semi-detached houses, Swiss Cottage at 35-37 St Andrews Drive, Pollokshields. James Boucher then built a similar Swiss Cottage for a holiday home at Coulport, Loch Long. Their business was quick to take off and together they worked on many designs which included the Gothic style Renfield Free Church on Bath Street, a large block of warehouses and shops at the corner of Gordon Street and Renfield Street (1857-58), the Romanesque Free Church at Kinning Park (1862-64) and plans for a considerable number of ambitious villas which were exhibited at the Royal Scottish Academy in 1860 and the Glasgow Institute in 1861.

Soon Walter MacFarlane of the Saracen Iron Works became a client and in addition to his warehouse in Washington Street (1862) and the Saracen Iron Works at Possilpark (begun 1869) they made many designs for architectural castings. The Cousland family had business connections with John Kibble whose father owned a wire and metal warehouse at Turner's Court on Argyle Street. In the early 1860s Kibble built a large Italian Romanesque villa called Coulport House opposite James Boucher's Swiss Villa at Loch Long. Kibble engaged the partners to design his conservatory which in enlarged form became the Kibble Palace in the Botanic Gardens. James Cousland is said to have made a model of the Kibble Palace in wire to show John Kibble what it would look like. The ironwork for the Kibble Palace was undertaken by John Boyd of Paisley. Sadly though, James Cousland`s career was to be short-lived. He witnessed a fatal accident during the building of the Free St. Georges Church and this greatly affected his health and contributed to his early decline. He died at his home Swiss Cottage, on 12 June 1866. James Boucher carried on the work of the company, and in 1875 went into partnership with one of his students Henry Higgins (also his assistant for two years). The firm then became known as Boucher & Higgins.

Continue along your route and just before you turn the corner you will see the large blonde sandstone monument to James Lindsay and family, adorned with rosettes and scallop shells. Scallop shells were carried by the pilgrims to the shrine of St James of Compostela but are purely decorative on this stone. The laying of scallop shells on graves was a common practice for many centuries. This free-standing double-panelled memorial is similar in size and design to many wall monuments, which you will see when you turn the next corner.

Dead You Know?

The Southern Necropolis is an enclosed graveyard and as such many monuments are to be seen on its walls. They range from a single gravestone to a series of panels with kerbstones enclosing the property of a family burial

*place. Many are elaborate in size and design and bear
evidence of polychromy: when monuments were erected
some were painted in a variety of colours. Over time
the paint layers have faded offering us only a glimpse
of what they must have looked like when first erected.
Also built into the walls of the Southern Necropolis are
relatively plain mural tablets. Usually made of sandstone
and rectangular in shape the mural tablet bears only an
inscription and little or no ornament. Over the years
erosion has taken its toll on these memorials and little or
no detail remains.*

**Continue to the next marker on your right. You will
be directed through the stones to the grey granite
headstone, with the carved relief of a sea rescue,
belonging to...**

12 James Banks McNeil (1831-1878) Lifesaver

James Banks McNeil was connected with boating and
swimming in Glasgow during the late 1800s. He built
boats, hired them out and was the founder and first
secretary of the City of Glasgow Regatta Club. At one
time he was a contender for the post of officer of the
Humane Society (presently held by George Parsonage).
An able and powerful swimmer he saved over 70
people from drowning. This resulted in his recognition
by the London Humane Society, who awarded him its
silver medal. James Banks McNeil was also a swimming
instructor in both Glasgow and Paisley and was
responsible for the building of Saint Andrew's Baths in

Greendyke Street. The baths were later converted into a used clothes market and eventually demolished.

When standing in front of the McNeil headstone, take a few steps back, mind your footing, and look for the grave marker to your right. Here you will find the red sandstone headstone bearing floral motifs which is the last resting place of…

13 John Begg (1796-1867) Nephew of Robert Burns

John was the son of Adam Begg and his wife, Isabella, was the youngest sister of Robert Burns. He was a farmer in Morvern in Argyll, and in his old age he and his wife moved to Rutherglen to live with their son.

In the Old Gorbals burial ground (now the Rose Garden) lies another local link to Robert Burns, a gentleman named John Wilson – the inspiration for the poem *Death and Dr Hornbook*. Wilson, in his early years as a schoolmaster at Tarbolton parish took to dabbling in amateur medicine by printing advertisements promoting his free advice for common ailments. After attending a Masonic meeting where John Wilson displayed his so-called medical skills, Robert Burns set about writing the verses for *Death and Dr Hornbook*.

Following the circulation of the poem John Wilson left Tarbolton and headed for Glasgow where he took up the position of session-clerk for the Gorbals Parish Church until his death in 1839.

This completes the eastern section.

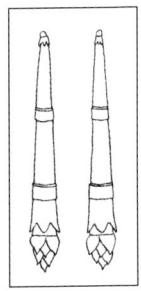

Return to the path and re-enter the central section, turning left as you enter. On the right hand side is the monument to Alexander Davidson with the hand and scroll symbolism of the recording angel with downward facing torches. Continue along the path to the next marker on the right which will direct you on a path through the stones to an ornate obelisk which is the grave of…

14 Charles Wilson (1810-1863) Architect

The son of a builder, Charles Wilson, served his architectural apprenticeship under the auspices of Glasgow architect David Hamilton. During the period from 1827 to 1837 he contributed to the design and building of Hamilton Palace, Lennox Castle and Toward Castle. In Glasgow, he worked with Hamilton on the conversion of the Cunningham Mansion into the Royal Exchange, which is now the Gallery of Modern Art. Charles Wilson left the David Hamilton practice in 1837 to enter into

partnership with his brother John. Their partnership ended in 1839 and Wilson set up his own practice at 41 George Square. The first two years saw him occupied with commissions to build a series of small churches and villas. In 1841 he was commissioned to design and build the Glasgow Royal Asylum for Lunatics at Gartnavel.

The 19th century offered great opportunities for young architects. As Glasgow extended its boundaries, huge areas of land were opened up to new development. One such development was the rocky outcrop of Woodlands Hill. The lower slopes of Woodlands Hill had been partially developed in the 1830s and the 1840s. However, by the 1850s, a proposed initiative to build the new university buildings on the summit had fallen through and Charles Wilson was commissioned to produce a plan for the Woodlands Hill and Park area. He entered into a joint venture with Sir Joseph Paxton and surveyor Thomas Kyle to produce a plan which would become Park Circus, Park Terrace and Kelvingrove Park.

The years following the Disruption of the Church of Scotland (1843) saw him build many Free Church buildings such as the Italianate style Free Church Training College on Lynedoch Street, Glasgow (1855-57) the Rothesay Free Church (1845), Maryhill Free Church (1847) and Rutherglen Free Church (1849), all built in different styles such as Romanesque and early English gothic.

The first mention of a gateway at the Southern Necropolis is found in a disposition dated 10 September 1844, by William Gilmour, to the Magistrates of Gorbals.

It mentions the rights of entry to the land disponed, by a road leading eastwards until it passes through 'the gateway with its accompanying ornaments to be erected in the centre.' This gateway still stands today at the entrance to the Southern Necropolis.

Turn around and face the path once again. Look a little to the right where you will see another grave marker identifying the grey granite monument to…

15 Reverend James E Smith (1801-1857) Preacher

James E Smith was born in Glasgow on the 22 November 1801, the son of John Smith of London and his wife Janet. His father, a well-educated man, had strong ambitions to see all his sons in the ministry. At the age of 17 he became a private tutor and probationer for the church and continued to teach within various families until 1829. Although preaching, he made no serious attempt to enter the church. After turning his talents to painting he managed to raise enough funds to take himself to London.

In 1832 he opened a chapel, charging 1d for admission. He circulated tracts and gave lectures. At first he had some success but, as the novelty of his views wore off, he then connected himself with Robert Owen, who developed New Lanark, and lectured at the Socialist Institution in Charlotte Street. Towards the end of August 1834, after a disagreement with Owen, James Smith established his own publication *The Shepherd* in which he discussed subjects that interested him.

After the publication ceased James turned his versatile hand to producing the *The Family Herald,* the first issue of which appeared in May 1843. This celebrated publication was sold weekly at the cost of 1d and was mainly devoted to popular fiction and was, according to the prospectus: 'The first specimen of a publication produced entirely by machinery, types, ink, paper and printing'. James 'Shepherd' Smith died in 1857. He is buried alongside his father and mother.

Four stones along to the right of Reverend Smith is the monument to Robert Reid which gives a superb example of lead lettering surrounded by a border of Celtic knotwork.

Dead You Know?

Inscriptions vary a great deal in lettering types and styles. Lettering can be 'incised' and sunk into the surface of the stone or 'in relief' to stand out from the surface. Bronze or lead sheet letters can also be attached to the stone. Lettering can also be applied using cast iron, lead or copper letters fixed with pins to the stone. (Vandals have caused damage to the surface of many of these stones by forcibly removing this lettering).

Inscriptions on early 16th and 17th century stones were in Latin whilst from the 18th century English was used, written in copperplate script. From the late 18th century onward the widespread use of calligraphy books made it easier to display individuality and ornament in inscriptions. The 19th century saw the introduction of the type book and with the publication of catalogues a variety of fonts and styles became widely available.

Continue along the path and on the left side against the wall you will see the sandstone pedestal tomb belonging to John Marshall with its high relief carving of mother and child. Further along and around the path you will find the next directional marker on the left hand side showing the site of an elaborate mural-like monument, bearing evidence of polychromy, of…

16 George Thomson (1815-1866) Shipbuilder

George Thomson was born on 25 March 1815 in Partick. His apprenticeship was as a millwright after which he entered the works of Robert Napier. Napier was a legendary engineer who also trained William Denny, John Elder and William Pearce. During his time there Thomson developed a considerable knowledge of marine and general engine work and his talents were soon recognised, leading to the position of assistant manager with the firm. In 1846, along with his older brother James, he started a successful engineering company at Clyde Bank Foundry in Govan, from which they set up a shipbuilding branch at Bankton, just east of Govan in 1851. The first ship that they produced was the *Mountaineer*, launched on 15 July 1852. This 175ft paddle steamer was constructed for use on the West Highland trade routes, then run by David Hucheson, and later David MacBrayne. Around 40 vessels were built in total, with names such as *Clansman*, *Columba* and *Claymore*.

During his lifetime George Thomson was deeply devoted to his business but was rarely seen or known in public. His yards employed more than 1500 men. The last ship designed by George Thomson was a 3,000 ton steam powered vessel named *Russia* in 1865, a mail ship for Cunard. At the time of its construction it was the largest and most important vessel operating on the Atlantic and was able to cross the ocean inside nine days. He died on 29 June 1866 aged 51. In 1871, his son James Roger Thomson purchased extensive lands at Barns of Clyde in Dunbartonshire, diagonally opposite the confluence with the Cart. The Govan yard and Thomson's entire operation was transferred across to the north bank of the Clyde, bringing with it the name Clyde Bank – later to be taken up by the town that grew around it. In 1899 Thomson's fine shipyard was taken over by John Brown and Company of Sheffield and became, arguably, the most famous shipbuilding yard on the River Clyde.

As you continue along the path towards the next corner you will see one of the many war graves in the Southern Necropolis.

Dead You Know?

Spread throughout the lairs of the Southern Necropolis there are many military memorial stones, with those commemorating the slaughter of men in the First World War outnumbering the rest. In excess of 100,000 British & Commonwealth war dead are buried in cemeteries across Britain. The majority lie in a Commonwealth War Grave each of which is uniquely marked with a simple and appropriate granite headstone, bearing the individual's name and regimental insignia.

Turn right at the next corner and just a few steps along is the next marker which directs you towards the bronze portrait and inscription in high relief encased in grey granite belonging to…

17 John Robertson (1782-1868) Marine Engineer

John Robertson was born on the 10 December 1782 in Neilston, Renfrewshire, the son of James Robertson, mill worker, a native of Stanley in Perthshire. John's career started at the age of 14 when he was apprenticed to Mr Cuthbertson, a spinning wheelwright in Neilston. After his apprenticeship he worked for two years as a turner at the Stanley Cotton Works in Perthshire before moving to Glasgow. For the following eight years he worked in the machine shop of William Dunn of Duntocher and John Street.

When his father died in 1810 he inherited a small engineering shop in Dempster Street, Glasgow. He entered into partnership with James Robertson (no connection) but the partnership dissolved within a year. His next partner John Ritchie left within two years and so he decided to soldier on alone.

He first met Henry Bell in 1808 when he was installing a small steam engine at Bell's Baths Hotel in

Helensburgh. By 1811, aged 29, John Robertson was a respected engineer and it is no surprise that after their initial meeting Bell chose his engine to power the near complete *Comet*. Robertson's double acting engine of 3 horse power was built to a modified beam engine design. It was installed on the vessel at her builders, John Wood and Company, Port Glasgow. Despite initial teething problems the *Comet* reached a speed of 5 knots on her trials.

The relationship between Robertson and Bell had become strained with the engineer advising Bell that the engine was too small and the arrangement of paddles unsatisfactory. There was further disagreement about the speed at which the engine should run. After only two months of service the *Comet* was withdrawn and Robertson installed a new cylinder and the two paddles at either side were replaced by a single paddle wheel at either side. Despite these improvements the *Comet* was unsuited for coastal work and on the 13 December 1820 the tide swept her onto Craignish Point where she was wrecked. The engine was salvaged and is now on display at The Science Museum at South Kensington, London.

The experience of the *Comet* convinced Robertson that there was a future for steam in marine propulsion and in 1813, with a new partner on board he had the *Clyde* built for him by Mr Wood for service between Glasgow, Greenock and Gourock. In 1814, the *Tay* was built for him by Mr Stuart of Dundee for which Robertson himself built and installed the engine. She ran for four years between Dundee and Perth and was later re-named the *Oscar* for service between Glasgow and Lochgoilhead. Mr Stuart also built the *Caledonia* and the *Humber* for service between Hull and Selby and Hull and Gainsborough respectively. All of this means that John Robertson was one of the first to export steam ships from Scotland. Mr Wood built two more ships for him, the *Defiance* in 1817 and the *Marquis of Bute* in 1818.

John Robertson never received the financial reward his work merited. His assets were tied up in steam ships and they were gradually disposed of at a considerable loss and by August 1826 he found himself in over £2000 of debt and was declared bankrupt. He eventually settled terms with his creditors and became dependant on the generosity of a few good friends. John Robertson died at Carrick Street, Glasgow on 19 November 1868. A memorial dedicated to his achievements was erected by parishioners and friends in his home town of Neilston on 24 August 1912. On the 22 April 1913 The Institution of Engineers and Shipbuilders in Scotland unveiled a memorial in the Southern Necropolis to mark the resting place of the Clyde's earliest marine engineer.

Return to the path and on your right hand side as you walk along you will notice the monument to compass maker John Fraser with its compass bearings and text. On the right side of the path as you walk towards the central circle there is a marker which will lead you to the gravestone of…

18 Captain James Smart (1804-1870) of the Glasgow Police

James Smart was born in Cathcart and spent his early years in Glasgow. As a young man he was employed for a short time in the tea trade in England but soon returned to Glasgow where in October 1831 he joined the Gorbals Police Force as a patrolman, gaining promotion to sergeant in 1832. In 1835, he was appointed as Superintendent of Calton Burgh Police. In 1846, when Calton, Gorbals and Anderston were annexed to Glasgow he was appointed Assistant Superintendent of the Eastern Division.

By 1848 distress, hunger and desperation were widespread. A slump in the textile trade had made thousands unemployed and the depression rapidly spread to other trades.

Meetings were held by the committees of the unemployed of all trades and crowds of over 7,000 gathered at Nelson's Monument at Glasgow Green. The result of one particular meeting saw peaceful crowds making their way to Bridgeton to bring out the mill workers in support. During the walk it was rumoured amongst the throng that the mills were being burnt. Police preparations had been made and the crowds were met at John Street (now Tullis Street) by James Smart with a number of Police and 17 Army pensioners who were armed with muskets. The people who gathered were now hemmed in as the order of 'Charge' was given by Smart (there was some confusion as to whether this meant 'attack' the crowd or 'load' muskets). The pensioners did neither, but fired into the crowd. Four men were killed and two more died later.

James Smart's reward for the handling of the crisis was promotion to the rank of Chief Superintendent in December 1848. In the Police Act of 1862, he was designated as Chief Constable of Police in Glasgow and his appointment led to many practical innovations. He was responsible for the introduction of the Mounted Branch and oversaw the abolition of the police rattle in favour of a whistle and the issue of batons in place of sticks. Another noteworthy innovation was the installation of the magnetic telegraph between police stations and fire stations. James Smart died on 27 May 1870.

Return to the path and turn to your left looking back along the path. Here you will notice a marker nearby on the opposite side which will direct you through the stones to the blonde sandstone monument belonging to…

19 Lt. R A Bogue MC (1888-1917) 16th Highland Light Infantry

Thiepval is a region in France close to the River Somme and was the site of one of the major battles of World War I, namely the Battle of the Somme. At 7.30am on the morning of 1 July 1916, at the River Somme, an artillery attack on the Germans attempted to destroy their barbed wire at various places and to hit them hard in their long line of deeply dug trenches. Even the explosion of several huge mines under the German front line did little to stop their machine-gunners cutting through the waves of British infantry on their way forward. On 15 September 1916 the British used tanks for the first time.

Only 40 tanks were available but very few of these

managed to reach the start line. At that time tanks were slower, less reliable and tactically too few in number to make an impact. The offensive lasted until the middle of November, leaving a landscape of cratered desolation and blood-filled pools.

Lieutenant Robert Alexander Bogue was severely wounded at the battle of Thiepval and died of his injuries 15 months later on the 26 September 1917. He is interred in New Kilpatrick (or Hillfoot) Cemetery, Bearsden but is fondly remembered on the family headstone and his name is included in the records of the War Graves Commission.

Dead You Know?

> *Included within the interment records of the Southern Necropolis are burials of 'legs' of individuals. Perhaps being the only part left following an industrial accident, or maybe that of someone who after having his limb amputated, felt it more respectful to have it buried.*

Return through the stones to the path and turn left walking towards the central circle. Turn left again and follow the path until you reach the next marker, which will direct you through the stones to a grave marker identifying the polished granite monument to…

20 James Salmon (1805-1888)
Architect

James Salmon was born on 11 October 1805, the son of John Salmon, a weaver and merchant from Bonhill, Dunbartonshire and Margaret Jackson. He was the second son to be named James, the first son having died at Christmas 1795. James moved to Glasgow at an early age and was married to Helen Russell (1817-1881) on 19 March 1837 in Edinburgh. They had five children – Wilhelmina born c1841; William Forest born 1843; Margaret born c1846; James born 19th June 1853 and Helen born 1856.

As an architect, Salmon was most famous for his work in the Italian Renaissance style, and his buildings include the Woodilee Asylum, the Magdalene Institution and the restoration of Paisley Abbey. He was also respected for his involvement in civic affairs. Salmon was elected to Glasgow Town Council in 1860. He was the first convenor of the Glasgow Libraries Committee. From the mid-19th century onwards the population of Glasgow grew rapidly and the needs of the city changed. The new working population urgently needed housing with as many houses as possible in as small a space as practical. At first the city merchants and new industrialists had their mansion houses in the city but soon wanted away from the smoke and clamour to new houses on the outskirts of Glasgow. Needs were changing along with a growth in civic pride. Glasgow was proud of its vitality and success and expected buildings of dignity and beauty. It was no wonder that the period produced great architects, one of whom was James Salmon.

James served his apprenticeship with architect John Brash who, between 1823-29, designed the houses of Blythswood Square. From 1841-43 Salmon and J Burnet were responsible for the beautiful high domed design of the Union Bank of Scotland, now known as the Corinthian Restaurant & Club at 191 Ingram Street. The interior includes allegorical statues from the mid to late Victorian period by John Mossman. Salmon was also the architect of the Lion Chambers in Hope Street. One of the great architectural opportunities of 19th century Glasgow came in the opening up of whole new areas for development and the freedom to design them. James Salmon's opportunity came with the planning of the new suburb of Dennistoun, a development commissioned by the wealthy entrepreneur Alexander Dennistoun (1790-1874). Between 1854 and 1861 Salmon designed, planned and supervised the development of the entire area, allegedly based on Paris, consisting of ornamental villas and self-contained houses mixed with terraces and open spaces. Unfortunately Salmon's original concept was much reduced and only Westercraigs remains with a few of the 'ornamental villas' and four terraces still in evidence from his stunning design, however the streets, terraces, drives and open spaces of this fine suburb remain as a testament to his genius.

As already indicated Salmon also designed the Barony Parochial Asylum at Woodilee. When it was opened in 1875 it was the largest parochial asylum in Scotland. Woodilee was the biggest employer in the area and had its own farms, fire brigade, sports and recreational facilities. At its height this vast institution accommodated over 1300 patients. Salmon was also the architect of Auchingramont Church in Hamilton which features a magnificent tall steeple. It was used for public worship from 1860 to 1980 when it was converted into flats. James Salmon wrote poetry and was Captain of the Glasgow Golf Club. He was the first president of the Glasgow Institute of Architects, his vice president being Alexander 'Greek' Thomson. He died on 5 June 1888, in his home at 3 Broompark Circus, Dennistoun.

His son James Salmon 2nd (1873-1924) known as the 'Wee Troot' was also a fine architect, best known for the Hatrack building at 142 St Vincent Street.

Return to the path and continue left along this route turning left just before the entrance to the western section. Continue to the next marker just past the cast iron monument.

Dead You Know?

In the 19th century many headstones were made of cast iron with raised designs and lettering. They came in a range of ornamental top shapes and open pattern work. However, many have succumbed to rust, making the inscriptions difficult to decipher. This particular example displays evidence of open pattern work with sandstone panelling which has either deteriorated over the years or has become prey to vandalism.

Just next to this on the left is the directional marker which will lead you through the stones once again to…

21 The White Lady

Of all the monuments in the Southern Necropolis one has gained a unique and mysterious reputation. It is the resting place of John S Smith, carpet manufacturer, his wife Magdalene and their housekeeper Mary McNaughton. In the form of a veiled woman beside a broken pillar, the much weathered memorial tells a fascinating story.

Although the date of her husband's death is no longer visible on the stone, the tragic story behind the accidental death of Magdalene and her housekeeper is poignantly told. On 29 October 1933 while returning from church to their home at Langside Avenue, sheltering from the heavy rain behind an umbrella, they walked into the path of a tramcar on Queen's Drive. Magdalene died on arrival at Victoria Infirmary and Mrs McNaughton passed away two weeks later. The monument is a solemn memorial to the tragedy. Local legend tells how the White Lady turns her head as you pass by. Of the braver among us who have ventured into the graveyard after dark a few come back to testify to a mysterious glow about the White Lady at dead of night.

The grand tombs of the 16th and 17th centuries made a feature of figures such as Faith, Hope and Charity and other personified Virtues and these were re-introduced in the Victorian period. The White Lady is the most obvious example of this feature in the Southern Necropolis. A full figure white marble portrait of a lady in mourning, symbolic of the earlier weepers, set on a granite pedestal and leaning against a broken column. The 19th century broken column shares symbolic similarity with the 18th century imagery of a broken tower representing the Day of Resurrection or similarly the destruction of the mortal world at the Day of Judgement. The broken column is a round column terminating in a jagged end and mounted on a pedestal and can be made from either sandstone or granite. The White Lady has become something of a local celebrity to generations of people from the Gorbals.

Dead You Know?

Local legend has it, that on arriving at the monument of the White Lady, you should run around her three times, shouting out loud 'White Lady! White Lady!' This will hopefully prevent her gaze from turning you to stone. If you wish to do so during the trail then take care that you don't catch her eye.

Return to the path and continue on your way left until you come to the next marker on the right. This is the last resting place of…

22 Allan Glen (1772-1850)
Wright and philanthropist

Allan Glen was the son of George Glen and Marion Mitchell who were married on 5 November 1771. The family farmed the lands of East Cowglen and Maudlans near Pollokshaws but the small size of the farm meant that it could barely support one family. This forced part of the family, including Allan Glen's parents, to move into Pollokshaws to find work. Pollokshaws at the end of the 18th century was a village with a population of around 2000 most of whom were employed in the cotton industry as spinners, weavers and bleachers. It seems likely that Allan Glen's parents had come to Pollokshaws to work in the weaving shops or spinning mills. Allan Glen himself was apprenticed to a carpenter.

In 1810, Allan Glen set up in business as a master wright in Glasgow but as he was from outwith the city he was obliged to seek admission to the Incorporation of Wrights. The Wrights of Glasgow had been granted a charter or Seal of Cause on 3 May 1600 to become a trade incorporation. Extensive and exclusive privileges were conferred upon the craft and new members who came from outside the city first had to gain admission to the relevant Trade Incorporation before

they were allowed to work within its boundaries. In more recent times the qualifications for gaining a burgess ticket have been much relaxed, but in Allan Glen's time the requirements were very strict and included a practical test.

The test was supervised by four examiners 'The Essay Masters'. Allan was given a block of rough wood and instructed to make a window, a bound shutter, a knife box, a footstool and a bound door. Then he was locked alone in the Essay Room until he completed the task. The work was examined by the Masters, and he passed. Finally, as a new member he would have to take an oath to be loyal to the Incorporation, maintain its standards and pay an entrance fee.

Allan Glen was one of the first members of the Unitarian Church which was established in 1808. Unitarians attached great value to education and Allan Glen reflected this in the foundation of his school. His business had prospered and when he died in 1850 he left money for two charity schools, one for boys and one for girls. They were to be non-sectarian and industrial, meaning they should provide a general basic education as well as the skills on which future trades might be built. Unfortunately, there was not enough money for the girls' school but the boys' school was built on ground belonging to Allan Glen at the corner of North Hanover Street and Cathedral Street. Allan Glen died of paralysis at his home in Gourock on the 18 February 1850.

Continue along the path, turn left at the corner and follow the route until you come to the next marker on the left hand side. Here you will find the monument to…

23 George Geddes (1826-1889)
Glasgow Humane Society

George Geddes was orphaned as a baby and was adopted by a family from Govan. At the age of seven he was sent to work 10 hours a day at a silk mill (in 1833 legislation for the protection of child workers was unknown).

In 1837 there was no St Andrew's Bridge at McNeil Street and a ferry took people across the river at that spot. George often helped his brother who was in charge of it. Aged 11 he saved a young girl from drowning which gave him a taste for rescuing people. He joined as an officer of the Humane Society in 1845 and in the first 15 years of his service saved no less than 35 lives. His dedication to lifesaving was recognised by the award of a gold medal by the Glasgow Society. As might be expected of someone who rescued people from a river George was an able oarsman. In a contest on Kilbirnie Loch he once beat the then famous Bob Campbell – Champion of Scotland. George died on 17th January 1889 aged 63. His family headstone includes the inscription 'A faithful public servant for 45 years and rescuer of over 100 persons'. His post was taken over by his son George II that same year. This important position with the Humane Society is held today by George Parsonage who himself took over from his late father Ben.

Just a few yards along on the right side of the path, overshadowed by a tree, is the lair of the Adshead family. This is an impressive monument with a highly polished grey granite coped stone adorned with a cross with its kerbstones still in place.

Return back along the path and enter the western section on the left hand side. Turn left and follow the path along and around. As you walk along the path you will notice on your left, just before the next marker, the grey granite headstone of Charles Thomson of the Glasgow Police Band. If you look closely you will see his helmet, trumpet and truncheon. Opposite Charles Thomson on the right side of the path is the monument to the Buckley family bearing the Victorian concept of a Weeper carved in full relief standing on top of a pedestal.

Continue to the next directional marker on the left side. The monument you are looking for is to the rear of the stone you are facing but if you pause for a moment and look to the right you will find the sandstone monument to the memory of Jane Hay.

Note the symbolic hand with a finger pointing to the heavens representing eternal life. Hands with pointing fingers can be used to indicate the inscription on a stone, and a hand showing the cuffs of a robe emerging from the clouds may represent the hand of God.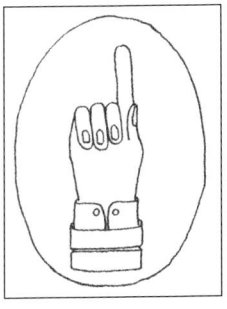

If you are indeed tempted to clamber over the fallen stones to the row behind then be careful not to trip or twist an ankle. Alternatively, you can walk to the gap in the stones and round to the row behind. Your heroics will lead you to the grave of…

24 Wee Willie White (d1858)
the blind flute and flageolet player

In a Glasgow so unlike the city we know today he was indeed a 'character' and well respected. Although not much has been recorded about this man his story is like many other 'deserving poor' – short and simple. He was below average height and his general appearance was somewhat squat but neither deformed nor repulsive. Entertaining his street audiences by playing popular and patriotic tunes he worked his talents from Jamaica Street to the Trongate. The small sums that he collected allowed him to live in what was then referred to as 'respectable poverty'. On 11 September 1858 while still by no means an old man he suddenly took ill on Glasgow Green. He lived long enough to be taken home to his lodgings at 102 Saltmarket where he died later that same day. His friends and admirers provided for his decent burial in the far left row in the western section of the Southern Necropolis, his resting place being marked by a simple headstone bearing a stone flute and the box in which it was carried.

This blonde sandstone monument to the blind street musician is one of the few examples of emblems of trade to be found in the Southern Necropolis, in this example the flute case which unfortunately is now bereft of its flute. Emblems of trade were very popular on 18th century monuments and examples of these are to be found in the nearby old Gorbals Burial Ground.

Dead You Know?

In 1954 over 100 local children gathered at the Southern Necropolis Gatehouse on Caledonia Road, each armed with stakes and crosses, word having spread that a youngster had been taken and eaten by a vampire with metal teeth. The police later arrived at the scene and dispersed the excited crowd. The following day the headline in the Evening Times read 'Vampire with Metal Teeth is Dead'.

Carefully make your way back onto the path and continue along to the next marker on the left hand side just before you reach the wall. Here you will notice an open space between the monuments. Follow the markers up and over the slope towards the grave marker of …

25 George Rodgers VC (1829-1870) of the 71st Regiment of Foot.

During the Indian Uprising, on 16 June 1858 at Marar, in India, Private George Rodgers single-handedly attacked a party of seven enemy soldiers, one of whom he killed. This was a particularly vital act of bravery as the enemy were all armed and posted in front of the line of advance of a detachment of the 71st Regiment.

Little is known of his life on return to Glasgow, but ironically, the manner of his death is recorded. It occurred in a bizarre accident 12 years later. Calling at his sister's house at 24 Govan Street, on the morning of 10 March 1870, George made repeated, unsuccessful attempts to obtain alcohol from her. She eventually persuaded him 'to have a lie down' instead. A short time later while she was out George got up and made his way into her kitchen where he found a bottle of what he thought contained spirits and promptly swallowed the contents. Unfortunately for him the bottle contained Vitriol (sulphuric acid), resulting in a painful death later that day. George was buried in 'accommodation ground'. This was a cheap grave that cost 36s 9d. It did not actually belong to one particular buyer and might be re-opened over several years.

Return to the path and continue forward with the wall on the left hand side. Just before turning right into the central pathway you will see the ornate Celtic cross to Neil McKelvie. Locals of a certain age tell the story of how a barrage balloon lost its moorings and became entangled on the cross of this stone during World War II. Continue round the corner and along through the central circle to the marker on the left next to the black Irish granite memorial to…

26 Alexander 'Greek' Thomson
(1817-1875)
Architect

Alexander Thomson was born in the Stirlingshire village of Balfron on 9 April 1817. His father John

Thomson was married twice, first to Christine Glass
with whom he had 8 children and then to Alexander's
mother, Elizabeth Cooper, with whom he had a further
11 children. Alexander was number 17. After the death
of his father in 1824 Alexander and those of his family
still living in Balfron moved to Glasgow to be near the
rest of the family. In Glasgow he trained as a lawyer's
clerk but his potential as an architect was soon to be
recognised by Glasgow architect Robert Foote who after
seeing some of his drawings made him an apprentice.
Robert Foote retired in 1836 and Alexander joined the
firm of John Baird I.

He left in 1849 to form a partnership with John Baird
II and their first buildings began to appear from 1850,
these included Seymour Lodge in Ardsloy, the Italian

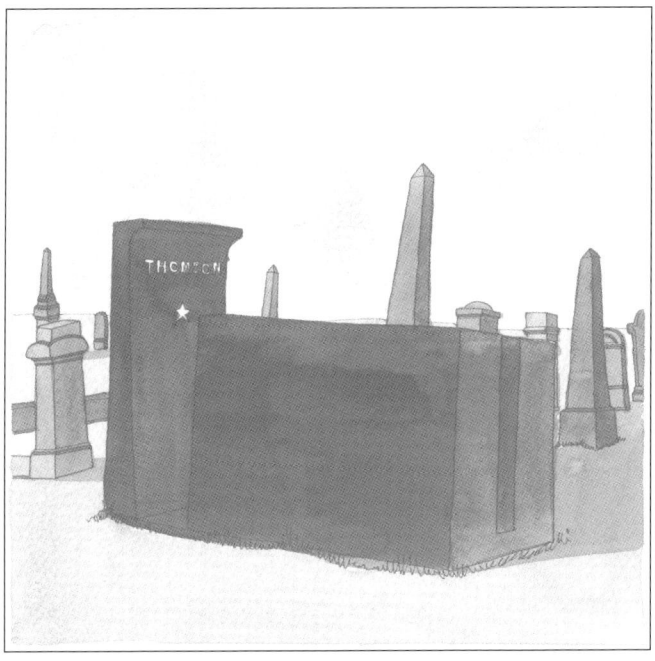

Villa in Cove and a series of villas in St Andrews Drive, Glasgow. There was more to their partnership than just business; they had married sisters, both of whom were the granddaughters of architect and writer Peter Nicholson, who designed Carlton Place. Alexander married Jane Nicholson and John Baird married her sister Jessie in a joint ceremony in London in 1847. Their home between 1849 and 1856 was a tenement building in Hutchesontown and from there the family moved to Shawlands and finally to Moray Place in 1860. In 1856 Alexander went into partnership with his brother George to form the company of A & G Thomson. As he concentrated more on design and draughtsmanship his style became more distinctive and his work included terraces, villas, churches and warehouses. It's not known when he was first given the soubriquet 'Greek' but his style was moving towards a modern interpretation of classical themes.

In 1870 his brother and partner, George, set out to fulfil a long held ambition by becoming a missionary in West Africa. George had run the business side of things and when Alexander entered into his last partnership with Robert Turnbull he must have been looking to him to take on George's role. After the death of his eldest child Agnes in 1854, Thomson purchased two lairs in the western section of the Southern Necropolis. Suffering for many years from asthma and bronchitis he found the cruel Glasgow winters hard to bear. He died at his home in Moray Place on 22 March 1875 aged 57. John Mossman, a leading sculptor, was commissioned to create a marble bust of Thomson, which can now been seen in Glasgow's Kelvingrove Museum.

Alexander Thomson was a founder member and president of the Glasgow Institute of Architects and in 1876, through fundraising by friends and fellow architects, the GIA established the Alexander Thomson Memorial. This was a travelling studentship to be awarded every three years to promote the study of classical architecture. In 1890, it was awarded to Charles Rennie Mackintosh. The studentship was revived as part of Glasgow's 1999 City of Architecture Festival. A competition was drawn up inviting entries for the design of a replacement monument for the grave of Alexander Thomson, the original having been removed through vandalism. The award was given to Glasgow based architecture students Graeme Andrew and Edward Taylor and was assembled by Watson Stonecraft. The polished black Irish granite monument was unveiled on 25 May 2006 by the Lord Provost of Glasgow, Liz Cameron, and attended by members of the Thomson Family.

Return to the central circle, turn right and continue along to the next corner. On your right, as you turn the corner, is the monument to William McKim of the Glasgow Savings Bank.

This sandstone Greek-style column has rusticated floral rope work running from the foot to the top. Rustication was a feature of the Victorian period and was a method whereby the surface of the stone was treated to produce an effect like wood, as in the shapes of logs.

Continue along the path to the first marker on the left hand side next to the blonde sandstone headstone of…

27 Cpt. Samuel B Murray (1862-1893) Ship's Captain

And to the right of that

28 William Hudson Birrell (1869-1893)

Both Captain Samuel B Murray and William Hudson Birrell drowned on board the passenger cargo vessel *SS Trinacria* when it sank off the coast of Spain on 8 February 1893.

The 2,256 ton steamship was built by Robert Duncan & Company of Port Glasgow in 1871, and her maiden voyage took place under the ownership of the Anchor Line in September of that year. The ship had accommodation for 69 1st and 910 3rd class passengers.

On 7 February 1893 she was wrecked north east of Cape Villano in Spain, having left Greenock on 2 February 1893 with 4 passengers and 37 crew, heading for the Mediterranean with Gibraltar the first port of call. With rough seas and poor visibility the ship was grounded 4 miles from the Cape Villano lighthouse, later capsizing from a massive burst of sea collapsing the funnels and ventilators onto the ship. In total 34 people lost their lives including the 4 passengers, three of whom were women missionaries bound for the garrison at Gibraltar and a young girl, who all drowned when the boat they were put into capsized after leaving the ship. The chief engineer, two seamen and four stokers were the only survivors.

This completes the western section.

Follow the path until you return to the entrance to central section once more. As you enter the central section, turn left and continue to the marker on the right hand side, which will direct you to the grey granite headstone of...

29 Robert Paterson (1820-1882) Vinegar Manufacturer

The Paterson family provided an essential item to Victorian households. Before the days of refrigeration the technique of pickling in vinegar was one of the few means of preserving food for any reasonable length of time, ensuring basic foods could be made available out of season. For example, the conscientious housewife would pickle eggs in the summer months when they were plentiful, for winter use. This of course also applied to tongues, hams, fruit and vegetables. Sheets soaked in vinegar were used to ward off infections from sick-rooms and after a long, tiring day the sniffing of vinegar could also help relieve headaches. These uses were wasted if the vinegar was not pure and merchants who sold it unadulterated were hard to find. However Robert had a good reputation for selling an honest product. His name appears regularly in the Post Office Directory from 1851 onwards.

In 1868 he was joined by his son Campbell and began to diversify into sauces, ketchup and fruit wines. Eight years later, following the death of its founder the Paterson Company was catapulted to fame with the first instant coffee: Camp Coffee (an essence of coffee-beans, chicory and sugar sold in a distinctive bottle). The

origin of Camp Coffee is believed to have come from a request from the Gordon Highlanders to Campbell Paterson for a coffee drink that could be used easily by the army on field campaigns in India. The regular process of grinding and brewing coffee beans was too complicated and time consuming for a military field kitchen. The creation of a liquid Camp Coffee provided a simpler method. The label of the product is said to bear the portrait of Sir Hector MacDonald, a hero of many wars in India. The Charlotte Street factory was founded in 1891 and the product proved so successful that three large additions were made between 1893 and 1908, in Charlotte Street and Greendyke Street. The Glasgow works closed in the 1970s and Camp coffee is now produced in Paisley.

Dead You Know?

A few yards along to the right of the Paterson monument is the blonde sand-stone memorial to William Campbell adorned with a symbolic hourglass in high relief, which represents the

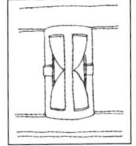

passing of time. The winged hourglass, which can also be seen in the Southern Necropolis represents the soul freed from the body winging its way to heaven and eternal life. Many other monuments not on the tour also bear symbolic carvings such as the winged cherub, often referred to as the winged soul, which represents the soul leaving the body at the time of death and making its ascent into heaven.

Another carving symbolic of mortality and immortality is the chrysalis and butterfly. The discarded chrysalis represents the end of mortal life and the butterfly represents the soul freed to an immortal life.

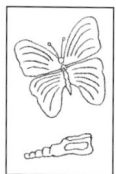

Return to the path and making your way towards the gatehouse you will see on your left hand side the wonderfully preserved cast iron headstone with sandstone panel of John Henderson, Collector of Police.

Part of his duties was to collect taxes for street lighting from local businesses.

Turn right at the gatehouse and walk along the central path until you come to the first marker on your right. The marker will direct you through the stones to the grave marker at the monument to…

30 Janet Jack, Bridget Ward & Margaret Jack Adams Higginbotham's Workers

These women lost their lives on the morning of 11 October 1895, in a fire at Higginbotham's & Company

Ltd, Calico Printers, McNeil St, Glasgow. The works covered a large area extending from McNeil Street to the River Clyde and had been the scene of several fires. A workforce of around 800 people, mainly women, was employed there at this time. It is thought that the fire started in the drying box. Cloth which came from the printing tables was passed through the drying box then on through an aperture and carried along the underside of a wooden floor. It was here that the cloth came within inches of the gas pendants, which lit the factory below.

The blaze took hold very quickly, passing through the three buildings fronting McNeil Street, shooting upwards to the top storeys and the roof. At first it was thought that everyone had escaped from the building, but soon the startling news spread that three women were missing; namely Janet Jack (36) of 271 Cumberland Street, Bridget Ward (18) of 263 Caledonia Street and Margaret Jack Adams (15) of 50 Old Dalmarnock Road. On entering the partially destroyed building the firemen discovered the remains of three bodies, which were taken to the mortuary at the Southern Police Office.

Return through the stones to the central path and continue towards the marker situated on the right. This is the final directional marker on the trail and it directs you to the grave of…

31 James Goldie (1844-1913) Brick Maker

James Goldie was born in Hutchesontown. His father James Goldie Senior was a brick-builder. He was educated at Gorbals Parish School. After leaving school at the age of 13, he spent the next six years acquiring knowledge of surveying at the offices of Shields and Duff, measurers, before he entered his father's business in 1863.

The work of Goldie & Son was linked to the growth of the city and at least two of the buildings for which they were responsible can be seen today – Fairfield's Yard at Govan and Templeton's Carpet Factory. Templeton's Factory, built in 1888 was designed by William Leiper. The intention was to reflect the brilliant colours of the carpets woven there in the exterior of the building, particularly the section derived from the Doge's Palace in Venice. The colours are crimson, red, deep blue, sand, white, green and yellow and the materials equally varied: brick, terracotta, enamel, sandstone and glazed bricks.

This was Goldie's masterpiece and for many years bricklayers' apprentices were brought to study the techniques he had used. Tragically on the 1 November 1889, during a heavy gale the back gable wall of the building collapsed killing 29 girls and injuring a further 22. After 1899 Goldie's interest changed to the politics of business and he became Dean of the Incorporation of Wrights and the following year he was elected Collector of the House. In 1903 he became Deacon-Convenor of the Trades House. After his term in office as Deacon-Convener he became manager of the Royal Infirmary and many other charitable institutions, such as Honorary President of the Building Trades Exchange which organised the great Scottish National Exhibition of 1911.

You have now reached the end of the
Southern Necropolis trail.

Post Script

We hope you enjoyed your tour of the Southern Necropolis. Membership of SGHET is open to everyone with an interest in the heritage of Glasgow. For further information contact Isobel Barrett:
Phone **0141 423 6037**
Email **chair@sghet.org**
Website **www.sghet.org**

If you would like to become involved with the Southern Necropolis project or book a free guided tour contact Colin Mackie:
Phone **0141 423 6037**
Email **colin@southernnecropolis.com**
Website **www.southernnecropolis.com**

For more information on the work of Adrian B McMurchie visit **www.adrian@amcmurchie.com**

SGHET would like to acknowledge the help and support of the following:
Isobel Barrett
Colin Mackie
Paul O'Cuinn
Adrian B McMurchie
Land Services, Glasgow City Council
Chief Executive's Office, Glasgow City Council
Mitchell Library, Culture and Sport Glasgow

Sources

Biographies

Nathaniel Paterson
> Thomson, J. History Of Old Saint Andrew's Parish Church. Glasgow 1905
> Cameron, John. The Parish Of Campsie. Kirkintilloch 1892
> Smout, T C. A History Of Scottish People

Peter Ferguson
> Aird, Andrew. Glimpses of Old Glasgow. Glasgow 1894

Tomas B Seath
> Murphy, William S. Captains Of Industry. Glasgow 1901
> Shearer, W Ross. Rutherglen Lore Paisley 1922

William 'Scotch' Williams
> Glasgow Herald, August 3rd 1842

Agnes Harkness
> Donaldson, Joseph. The Eventful Life of A Soldier Edinburgh, 1841, 1865
> Littell's Living Age, Vol. III, 1844

William Cameron
> Cameron, William. Manuscript of Songs & Poems
> Pawnbrokers Trade Circular 1872
> Rogers, Charles. The Modern Scottish Minstrel, Edinburgh 1855-58

Sir Thomas Lipton
> Lipton, Thomas. Leaves from the Lipton Logs. London 1931
> Forrest, Denys. The World Tea Trade. Cambridge 1985

Archibald Sinclair
> Report of the Proceedings/Annual Meeting of the Islay Association (October 30th 1878) Souvenir Programme/ Glasgow Islay Association (March 14th 1924)
> Museum of Islay Life, Port Charlotte, Isle of Islay.

James Cousland
> Dictionary of Scottish Architects
> www.codexgeo.co.uk/dsa/architect

James Banks McNeil
> Glasgow Herald, October 12th 1878

John Begg
> www.robertburns.org

Charles Wilson
    Gomme A & Walker A. Architecture of Glasgow. London 1968
    Worsdall, Frank. Victorian City. Glasgow 1992
George Thomson
    Memoirs and Portraits of 100 Glasgow Men. Glasgow 1886
    Glasgow Digital Library http://gdl.cdlr.strath.ac.uk/mlemen/
John Robertson
    Glasgow Corporation & the Clyde Navigation Trust Comet
    Centenary 1812-1912 Glasgow 1912
James Smart
    Minutes of Evidence from the Enquiry into the Conduct and
    efficiency of the Police during the late riots 1848.
    Glasgow 1848.
    Few incidents in the life of John Andrews, late Secretary of
    the Committee of Unemployed Trades of Glasgow. Glasgow, 1848
James Salmon
    Dictionary of Scottish Architects
    www.codexgeo.co.uk/dsa/architect
The White Lady
    Article covering the tram accident of Magdelene Blair &
    Mary McNaughton. Daily Record October 30th 1933
Allan Glen
    The Incorporation of Wrights in Glasgow 5th ed. 1928
George Geddes
    Geddes Family Papers. Glasgow City Archives. TD 249
Wee Willie White
    MacKenzie, Peter. Glasgow Characters. Glasgow 1857
George Rodgers
    Glasgow Herald, March 7th 1870
Alexander Greek Thomson
    McFadzean, Ronald. The Life and Work of Alexander
    Thomson. London 1979
    Stamp, Gavin & McKinstry, Sam Greek Thomson Edinburgh
    1994
Capt. Samuel B Murray and William Hudson Birrell
    Glasgow Herald, February 10th 1893, report of the sinking of
    SS Trinacria

Paterson Family (Camp Coffee)
    Glasgow Post Office Directory
    The Grocer Supplement for the Grocery Exhibition
    September 28th 1901
Janet Jack, Bridget Ward and Margaret Jack Adams
    Glasgow Herald, October 12th 1895, Article covering the fire
    at Higginbothams Mill, McNeil Street

Historical

Excerpt from disposition by the trustees of the deceased William
Gilmour esq., merchant in Glasgow to the magistrates of
Gorbals in trust within mentioned. 10 September 1844.
Glasgow University Archives (GUA 13098)
Chadwick E
    Practice of interments in towns, London 1843
Mitchell, John Oswald
    Old Glasgow Essays. Glasgow 1905
Reid, Robert
    Glasgow Past and Present. Glasgow 1894
Brotchie, T C F
    History of Govan. Govan 1905
Renwick, R & Lindsay, J
    History of Glasgow. Glasgow 1921
Renwick, R
    Early Glasgow. Glasgow 1911
Willsher Betty
    Understanding Scottish Graveyards. Edinburgh 1985
Willsher, Betty
    Scottish epitaphs; epitaphs and images from Scottish
    Graveyards Edinburgh 1996
Cunningham, J M
    Western Southern Necropolis: a statement of dispute between
    the lair holders and Mr W J Edmiston, presumed proprietor.
    Glasgow c 1869
Hutt, Charlotte
    City of the dead: the story of Glasgow's Southern Necropolis,
    Glasgow 1996

Petitions by the sanitary department for the closure of certain
burying grounds 1870-76. Glasgow City Archives (D-TC6/317)

Glaister, John
The epidemic history of Glasgow during the century
1783-1863. Glasgow 1886

Laurie, David,
Memorial respecting the parishes of Govan and Gorbals.
Glasgow 1826
Decreet of disjunction and new erection, the feuers of Gorbals
against the minister and heritors of Govan, 1771. Glasgow

MacLeod, K M
Report on the burial grounds in Glasgow. Glasgow 1878

Ferguson T
Scottish social welfare 1864 -1914. Edinburgh 1958

Gorbals cemetery.
Notes on the community and burying ground: report of
sub-committee on burying ground, 1885. Glasgow
City Archives (D-TC6/317)

Augmentation of Gorbals living by James MacLean, minister
versus the bailies of the village of Gorbals, 1824.
Glasgow City Archives (D-TC6/551)

Law papers: A H and Company. The Mitchell Library

Lees, R E M
Epidemic disease in Glasgow during the 19th century in
Scottish Medical Journal, 1996

Russell, J B
The policy and practice of Glasgow in the management of
epidemic diseases with results, 1881.

Ord, John
The story of the barony of Gorbals. Paisley 1919

Gorbals Burying Ground: Cases decided in the Court of Session,
Teind Court, Court of Exchequer and House of Lords: Scotch
Courts from Nov 17 1858 to July 20 1859.

Session Cases, Dunlop 1858-59. Glasgow City Archives (LR: 21D.104)

Gordon, J F S The history of Glasgow. Glasgow 1872

Cleland James. Annals of Glasgow. 1816

Gourlay, James A Glasgow Miscellany. Glasgow c1855.
The Regality Club. Proceedings. Glasgow 1889& 1893
The New Statistical Accounts for Scotland, Vol. VI.
Edinburgh, 1835